# It's in the Bag

We selected a variety of healthful recipes that are delicious and easy to prepare—*and* portable. Recipes include grab-and-go breakfast muffins and quick-to-assemble wraps that can be eaten out of hand, as well as hot soups and crunchy salads— all perfect for lunch at your desk, at work, or on the move. Most of the recipes can be prepared, packaged, and refrigerated the night before. So the next morning you can just pack the lunch bag and head out the door!

## A few simple tips will help you keep the contents of your lunch bag safe.

• **Prepare your lunch on a clean surface.** Wash your hands and clean the area before preparing food. Be sure to thoroughly wash packing materials—such as the insulated lunch bag and thermos—after each use.

• **Maintain proper food temperature.** An insulated lunch bag will keep your food fresh longer than a brown bag. If you do not have access to a refrigerator, put an ice pack or frozen drink in the bag to make sure your food stays cold.

• **Keep hot foods hot.** Heated liquids, such as soup, should be sealed tightly in a thermos. Rinse the empty thermos with boiling water, and then immediately pour the liquid into it; your meal should stay warm and tasty until lunchtime.

# Strawberries and Cream Cheese–Filled Muffins

A slather of fruit and cream cheese on top of a muffin is too messy to eat on the run—so we tucked the goodies inside. For variety, try different flavors of preserves. This recipe can be doubled or tripled to feed a family for an entire week.

¼  cup (2 ounces) ⅓-less-fat cream cheese, softened
2  tablespoons strawberry preserves
2¼  cups all-purpose flour
⅓  cup sugar
2  teaspoons baking powder
2  teaspoons poppy seeds
½  teaspoon baking soda
¼  teaspoon salt
1¼  cups low-fat buttermilk
3  tablespoons vegetable oil
2  large egg whites
1  large egg
Cooking spray

**1.** Preheat oven to 375°.
**2.** Combine cream cheese and preserves; stir with a whisk.
**3.** Lightly spoon flour into dry measuring cups; level with a knife. Combine flour and next 5 ingredients in a medium bowl; make a well in center of mixture. Combine buttermilk, oil, egg whites, and egg; stir well with a whisk. Add to flour mixture, stirring just until moist.
**4.** Spoon batter into 12 muffin cups coated with cooking spray, filling one-third full.
**5.** Top each with about 1 teaspoon cream cheese mixture; divide remaining batter evenly over cream cheese mixture. Bake at 375° for 25 minutes or until muffins spring back when touched lightly in center. Remove muffins from pans immediately; place on a wire rack. Yield: 1 dozen (serving size: 1 muffin).

CALORIES 182; FAT 5.9g (sat 1.7g, mono 1.6g, poly 2g); PROTEIN 5g; CARB 27.4g; FIBER 0.7g; CHOL 23mg; IRON 1.3mg; SODIUM 231mg; CALC 94mg

Make-Ahead Tip: Muffins can be stored in an airtight container overnight. Or place them in a zip-top plastic bag in the freezer; just thaw at room temperature, and eat.

# Chewy Coconut-Granola Bars

For an energy boost that stays with you until dinner and tempers your appetite, take a moment for this grain and fruit–filled snack.

Cooking spray
- 2 teaspoons all-purpose flour
- ⅔ cup all-purpose flour
- ⅓ cup whole wheat flour
- 1 teaspoon baking powder
- ½ teaspoon salt
- 1¼ cups packed brown sugar
- ¼ cup vegetable oil
- 2 tablespoons fat-free milk
- 2 large eggs
- 1½ cups low-fat granola without raisins (such as Kellogg's)
- ¾ cup chopped dried mixed fruit (such as Marian Premium Tropical Medley)
- ½ cup flaked sweetened coconut

**1.** Preheat oven to 350°.
**2.** Coat a 13 x 9-inch baking pan with cooking spray; dust with 2 teaspoons all-purpose flour. Lightly spoon ⅔ cup all-purpose flour and whole wheat flour into dry measuring cups; level with a knife. Combine flours, baking powder, and salt in a small bowl, stirring with a whisk. Combine brown sugar, oil, milk, and eggs in a large bowl; beat at high speed of a mixer until smooth. Add flour mixture, beating at low speed until blended. Fold in granola and fruit. Spoon batter into prepared pan. Sprinkle with coconut. Bake at 350° for 20 minutes or until golden. Cool on a wire rack. Yield: 20 servings (serving size: 1 bar).

CALORIES 157; FAT 4.7g (sat 1.6g, mono 1.2g, poly 1.5g); PROTEIN 2.1g; CARB 27.8g; FIBER 1.1g; CHOL 22mg; IRON 1mg; SODIUM 122mg; CALC 34mg

Make-Ahead Tip: Wrap each bar in plastic wrap, and store in an air-tight container; then the bars will be ready to toss into your lunch bag.

# Hummus Spread

This flavorful spread adds a taste of the exotic to a regular sandwich.

½ cup 1% low-fat cottage cheese
¼ cup fresh parsley leaves
2 tablespoons tahini (sesame-seed paste)
¼ teaspoon grated lemon rind
1 tablespoon fresh lemon juice
½ teaspoon ground coriander
⅛ teaspoon salt
1 garlic clove
1 (15½-ounce) can chickpeas (garbanzo beans), rinsed and drained

**1.** Place all ingredients in a food processor; process until smooth, scraping sides of processor bowl once. Store in an airtight container in refrigerator. Serve with pita triangles or fresh vegetables. Yield: 4 servings (serving size: ½ cup).

CALORIES 184; FAT 6.1g (sat 0.9g, mono 2g, poly 2.5g); PROTEIN 11.2g; CARB 22.7g; FIBER 3.4g; CHOL 1mg; IRON 3mg; SODIUM 342mg; CALC 92mg

# Citrus Salad

We used refrigerated orange sections, but you can substitute refrigerated pink and white grapefruit sections.

1 cup refrigerated orange sections
2 teaspoons olive oil
2 teaspoons balsamic vinegar
6 cups mixed salad greens
¼ cup chopped red onion
¼ teaspoon freshly ground black pepper

**1.** Drain orange sections, reserving 2 tablespoons juice. Combine reserved orange juice, olive oil, and vinegar, stirring with a whisk.
**2.** Combine salad greens, orange sections, and onion; add vinaigrette, and toss gently. Sprinkle with pepper. Yield: 4 servings (serving size: 1½ cups).

CALORIES 64; FAT 2.6g (sat 0.4g, mono 1.7g, poly 0.3g); PROTEIN 1.9g; CARB 9.9g; FIBER 3.1g; CHOL 0mg; IRON 1.2mg; SODIUM 22mg; CALC 67mg

# Cantaloupe with Raspberry–Poppy Seed Dressing

Store the dressing in a separate container, and pour over the cantaloupe just before serving. If you prefer, cut the cantaloupe into chunks; or purchase precut cantaloupe in the deli or refrigerated section of the supermarket.

  1/4  cup raspberry wine vinegar
1 1/2  tablespoons honey
    1  teaspoon poppy seeds
    1  cantaloupe, cut into 4 slices

**1.** Combine vinegar, honey, and poppy seeds, stirring well; drizzle over cantaloupe. Yield: 4 servings (serving size: 1 slice cantaloupe and about 1 tablespoon dressing).

CALORIES 78; FAT 0.3g (sat 0g, mono 0g, poly 0.2g); PROTEIN 1.2g; CARB 18.8g; FIBER 1.1g; CHOL 0mg; IRON 0.6mg; SODIUM 27mg; CALC 31mg

# Fresh Fruit Salad

Spoon the fruit mix into individual 1-cup plastic storage containers; chill overnight. Serve as a salad or light dessert with lunch or as a quick afternoon snack.

  2  cups blueberries
  1  cup sliced strawberries
  1  cup sliced peeled kiwifruit (about 3)
1/4  cup pineapple juice

**1.** Combine all ingredients; toss gently. Yield: 4 servings (serving size: 1 cup).

CALORIES 100; FAT 0.7g (sat 0g, mono 0g, poly 0.2g); PROTEIN 1.6g; CARB 24.5g; FIBER 4.1g; CHOL 0mg; IRON 0.7mg; SODIUM 1.7mg; CALC 34mg

# Romaine–Greek Vegetable Salad

Add the dressing just before eating so that the veggies stay crispy and fresh.

- 4 cups packaged torn romaine lettuce
- 1 cup presliced mushrooms
- ¼ cup thinly sliced red onion
- 1 teaspoon dried oregano
- 16 grape tomatoes, halved
- 12 coarsely chopped pitted kalamata olives
- 1 (15½-ounce) can chickpeas (garbanzo beans), rinsed and drained
- 1 cucumber, peeled and chopped
- ¼ cup low-fat Italian dressing
- 1 (4-ounce) package crumbled feta cheese with basil and sun-dried tomatoes

**1.** Combine first 8 ingredients in a large bowl; toss gently. Add dressing and cheese just before serving; toss gently. Yield: 4 servings (serving size: 2 cups).

CALORIES 226; FAT 9g (sat 4.7g, mono 2.6g, poly 0.9g); PROTEIN 10.7g; CARB 28.1g; FIBER 6.6g; CHOL 26mg; IRON 3.5mg; SODIUM 872mg; CALC 232mg

# Pita Crisps

This recipe is easily doubled so that you'll always have crisps on hand. Store in an airtight container up to 1 week.

- ¼ teaspoon garlic powder
- ¼ teaspoon onion powder
- ¼ teaspoon salt
- ⅛ teaspoon ground red pepper
- 2 whole wheat pitas, each cut into 8 wedges

Cooking spray

**1.** Preheat oven to 450°.
**2.** Combine first 4 ingredients. Coat pita wedges with cooking spray; sprinkle evenly with spice mixture. Bake at 450° for 4 minutes or until crisp. Yield: 4 servings (serving size: 4 crisps).

CALORIES 86; FAT 0.8g (sat 0.1g, mono 0.1g, poly 0.3g); PROTEIN 3.2g; CARB 17.9g; FIBER 2.4g; CHOL 0mg; IRON 1mg; SODIUM 316mg; CALC 6mg

Quick Tip: Use scissors or kitchen shears to cut the pitas into wedges.

# Lunch Menu
## SERVES 6

Serve Cuban Beans-and-Rice Salad as a side for dinner and take leftovers to work. You can make the salsa ahead and keep it refrigerated. But since it can become spicier as it sits overnight, you may want to cut back on the jalapeño. Use fresh pineapple for the best flavor.

### Cuban Beans-and-Rice Salad
Pineapple Salsa *
baked tortilla chips

* **Place** 3 cups chopped pineapple, 2 tablespoons chopped green onions, 2 teaspoons chopped fresh jalapeño pepper, 2 teaspoons chopped fresh mint, 1 teaspoon chopped fresh cilantro, 1 teaspoon fresh lime juice, ¼ teaspoon ground cumin, and ⅛ teaspoon salt in a medium bowl. Toss to combine.

## Cuban Beans-and-Rice Salad

½ cup diced peeled avocado
2 tablespoons balsamic vinegar
1 tablespoon olive oil
1 teaspoon ground cumin
½ teaspoon salt
¼ teaspoon black pepper
3 cups cooked white rice
1 cup chopped seeded plum tomato (about 3)
¼ cup minced fresh parsley
1 (15-ounce) can black beans, rinsed and drained
2 tablespoons minced fresh cilantro (optional)

**1.** Combine first 6 ingredients in a bowl; toss gently. Add rice, next 3 ingredients, and, if desired, cilantro; toss well. Serve chilled or at room temperature. Yield: 6 servings (serving size: 1 cup).

CALORIES 184; FAT 4.6g (sat 0.7g, mono 3g, poly 0.5g); PROTEIN 4.9g; CARB 32.8g; FIBER 4g; CHOL 0mg; IRON 2.3mg; SODIUM 421mg; CALC 36mg

# Ham-and-Rice Salad with Spinach

Assemble this great salad for tomorrow's lunch while you cook tonight's supper. The hearty serving size guarantees that the salad will always be a welcome lunchtime meal.

1½  cups water
 ⅔  cup uncooked fast-cooking recipe long-grain and wild rice (such as Uncle Ben's)
 ¼  cup sweetened dried cranberries (such as Craisins)
 4  cups chopped spinach leaves
 1  cup diced cooked ham
 ¼  cup chopped red onion
 2  teaspoons olive oil
 1  (11-ounce) can mandarin oranges in light syrup, undrained

**1.** Bring 1½ cups water and rice to a boil in a saucepan. Cover, reduce heat, and simmer 22 minutes. Stir in cranberries; cover and cook 2 minutes. Remove from heat. Let stand, covered, 5 minutes or until liquid is absorbed. Cool. Combine rice mixture, spinach, and remaining ingredients in a large bowl; toss well. Store in an airtight container in refrigerator. Yield: 2 servings (serving size: 2 cups).

CALORIES 451; FAT 14.2g (sat 3.6g, mono 7.5g, poly 1.6g); PROTEIN 20.7g; CARB 49.8g; FIBER 6.3g; CHOL 48mg; IRON 5.4mg; SODIUM 1,229mg; CALC 146mg

Quick Tip: Packaged long-grain and wild rice mixes speed up the cooking time and ease the expense of traditional wild rice.

## Orzo Salad with Corn, Tomatoes, and Basil

The tiny pasta soaks up the vinaigrette as the dish stands. Short tube-shaped macaroni, called ditalini, or small shells also work well in this recipe.

**DRESSING:**
- 2 tablespoons fresh lemon juice
- 1 tablespoon olive oil
- 1 teaspoon red wine vinegar
- ½ teaspoon salt
- ¼ teaspoon black pepper
- 3 garlic cloves, crushed

**SALAD:**
- 1 cup uncooked orzo (rice-shaped pasta)
- 2 cups fresh yellow corn kernels (about 4 ears)
- 2 cups chopped tomato
- ½ cup vertically sliced red onion
- ¼ cup finely chopped fresh basil

**1.** To prepare dressing, combine first 6 ingredients in a jar; cover tightly, and shake vigorously.

**2.** To prepare salad, cook pasta according to package directions, omitting salt and fat. Drain and place in a large bowl. Spoon half of dressing over pasta; toss to coat. Cool to room temperature. Add remaining dressing, corn, tomato, onion, and basil to pasta mixture; toss to coat. Let stand 30 minutes. Yield: 4 servings (serving size: about 1½ cups).

CALORIES 312; FAT 5.4g (sat 0.8g, mono 3g, poly 1.2g); PROTEIN 10.1g; CARB 59g; FIBER 5.1g; CHOL 0mg; IRON 2.9mg; SODIUM 318mg; CALC 27mg

# Thai Shrimp-and-Pasta Salad

Store the shrimp-and-pasta mixture and vinaigrette separately in the refrigerator; toss just before serving. Bottled fish sauce is a salty condiment that accounts for the high sodium content of this salad. It's sometimes labeled *nam pla* in Asian markets or your supermarket's ethnic-food section.

  2  ounces uncooked linguine
  ½  cup shredded carrot
  ½  pound medium shrimp, cooked and peeled
  1  cup thinly sliced Boston lettuce leaves
  ¼  cup fresh cilantro leaves
  2  tablespoons chopped unsalted, dry-roasted peanuts
  ¼  cup fresh lime juice
  2  tablespoons chopped fresh cilantro
  2  tablespoons fish sauce
  1  tablespoon chopped green onions
2½  teaspoons sugar
  2  teaspoons vegetable oil
  1  teaspoon grated peeled fresh ginger
  2  garlic cloves, minced

**1.** Cook pasta in boiling water 9½ minutes, omitting salt and fat. Add carrot; cook an additional 30 seconds. Drain and rinse with cold water. Combine pasta mixture, shrimp, lettuce, cilantro leaves, and peanuts in a large bowl; toss well.

**2.** Combine lime juice and remaining 7 ingredients in a jar. Cover tightly, and shake vigorously. Pour over pasta mixture, tossing gently to coat. Yield: 2 servings (serving size: 2 cups).

CALORIES 367; FAT 10.6g (sat 2g, mono 3.8g, poly 4.8g); PROTEIN 26.2g; CARB 37.4g; FIBER 3.2g; CHOL 166mg; IRON 4.9mg; SODIUM 1,512mg; CALC 80mg

Quick Tip: To save preparation time, purchase cooked and peeled shrimp at the seafood market or seafood counter in the supermarket. You'll need ½ pound of shrimp for the salad.

# Pasta-Chicken Salad
## with Fresh Vegetables

This pasta salad is best made ahead to give the flavors time to blend. The mix of the lemon-and-dill dressing with the tender chicken and crunchy fresh vegetables is very satisfying. Serve with reduced-fat cheddar cheese slices and buttery crackers to fuel you up for the rest of the day without having to spend much time preparing lunch.

1 ½   cups uncooked fusilli (short twisted spaghetti)
1   cup chopped cooked chicken breast
⅓   cup chopped celery (about 1 stalk)
1   cup grape tomatoes
1   cup chopped seeded cucumber (about 1 medium)
½   cup (2 ounces) crumbled light feta cheese
¼   cup fat-free lemon-and-dill dressing
¼   teaspoon salt
¼   teaspoon coarsely ground black pepper

**1.** Cook pasta according to package directions, omitting salt and fat; drain and rinse with cold water. Drain well.
**2.** Combine cooled pasta and remaining ingredients; toss gently to coat. Chill 2 hours. Yield: 4 servings (serving size: 1 ⅓ cups).

CALORIES 226; FAT 4.1g (sat 1.8g, mono 0.2g, poly 0.4g); PROTEIN 18.7g; CARB 29.3g; FIBER 2.0g; CHOL 35mg; IRON 1.5mg; SODIUM 425mg; CALC 82mg

Make-Ahead Tip: After the salad has chilled 2 hours, divide evenly into individual sized airtight containers and refrigerate for meals that are ready to go.

# Pizza Pasta Salad

Stir in your favorite pizza toppings, such as green pepper strips, onions, and mushrooms.

|   |   |
|---|---|
| 8 | ounces uncooked rotini (corkscrew pasta) |
| 1 | (14-ounce) can quartered artichoke hearts, drained |
| 6 | ounces cubed part-skim mozzarella cheese |
| 2 | cups grape tomatoes, halved |
| 4 | ounces sliced turkey pepperoni |
| ¼ | cup sliced ripe olives |
| 1 | (12-ounce) bottle roasted red bell peppers, drained |
| ⅓ | cup reduced-fat Italian dressing |
| ½ | cup thinly sliced fresh basil |
| ¼ | teaspoon freshly ground black pepper |

**1.** Cook pasta according to package directions, omitting salt and fat. Drain and rinse under cold water. Place drained pasta in a large serving bowl.

**2.** Combine artichoke hearts and next 4 ingredients; set aside.

**3.** Place roasted peppers in a blender, and process until almost smooth. Stir in dressing, basil, and black pepper.

**4.** Add pepper mixture and artichoke mixture to pasta; toss well. Yield: 6 servings (serving size: 1⅔ cups).

CALORIES 323; FAT 10.9g (sat 3.8g, mono 2.9g, poly 1.1g); PROTEIN 19.7g; CARB 36.5g; FIBER 3.8g; CHOL 40mg; IRON 2.6mg; SODIUM 1,074mg; CALC 218mg

Make-Ahead Tip: Prepare this salad the day before, and then cover and store it in the refrigerator until serving time.

# Grilled Chicken Salad with Sesame Seed Vinaigrette

Rather than heat up the grill to cook the chicken, substitute 1 (6-ounce) package grilled chicken strips from the meat department of most supermarkets.

2 (6-ounce) skinless, boneless chicken breast halves
¼ teaspoon salt, divided
¼ teaspoon pepper, divided
Cooking spray
3 cups prepackaged fresh baby spinach
½ cup seedless red grapes, halved
2 teaspoons sesame seeds, toasted
1 tablespoon red wine vinegar
3 tablespoons unsweetened white grape juice
2 teaspoons sesame oil

**1.** Prepare grill.
**2.** Sprinkle chicken evenly with ⅛ teaspoon each of salt and pepper. Place chicken on grill rack coated with cooking spray; grill 5 to 7 minutes on each side or until done.
**3.** Combine spinach, grapes, and sesame seeds in a large bowl. Combine vinegar, juice, oil, and ⅛ teaspoon each of salt and pepper.
**4.** Slice chicken diagonally into thin slices. Toss chicken with spinach mixture. Drizzle vinaigrette over salad before serving. Yield: 2 servings (serving size: 3 ounces chicken and 1½ cups salad).

CALORIES 231; FAT 7.7g (sat 1.1g, mono 2.2g, poly 2.4g); PROTEIN 28.6g; CARB 13.7g; FIBER 2.7g; CHOL 66mg; IRON 2.5mg; SODIUM 406mg; CALC 68mg

Quick Tip: To freshen and crisp bagged spinach, rinse and toss it in a salad spinner just before serving

# Roasted Red Bell Pepper Spread Sandwiches

### (cover recipe)

If you like pimiento cheese, you'll enjoy this recipe. Keep the sandwiches well chilled so that the cream cheese spread remains firm. Sturdy, whole grain bread works best.

½  cup finely chopped seeded cucumber
1  (7-ounce) bottle roasted red bell peppers, drained and finely chopped
¾  cup (6 ounces) ⅓-less-fat cream cheese, softened
⅓  cup (3 ounces) block-style fat-free cream cheese, softened
3  tablespoons minced red onion
¼  teaspoon salt
1  garlic clove, minced
8  (1½-ounce) slices whole grain bread
8  romaine lettuce leaves

**1.** Spread cucumber and peppers onto several layers of heavy-duty paper towels; let stand 5 minutes to drain excess moisture. Scrape into a medium bowl using a rubber spatula. Add cheeses, onion, salt, and garlic; stir with a fork until well blended. Spread about ½ cup cheese mixture over 4 bread slices; top each serving with 2 lettuce leaves and 1 bread slice. Yield: 4 servings (serving size: 1 sandwich).

CALORIES 356; FAT 11.9g (sat 6.4g, mono 2.9g, poly 0.4g); PROTEIN 14.9g; CARB 43.6g; FIBER 4.1g; CHOL 36mg; IRON 2.9mg; SODIUM 875mg; CALC 173mg

Quick Tip: To seed a cucumber quickly, cut it in half lengthwise and use the tip of a spoon or a melon baller to scoop out the seeds.

## Herb-Marinated Fresh Mozzarella Wraps

Pepper ham is available in the deli section of most supermarkets. If you're unable to find it, substitute regular ham and add ¼ teaspoon freshly ground pepper to the cheese as it marinates.

¾  cup (3 ounces) diced fresh mozzarella cheese
2  tablespoons chopped fresh basil
2  tablespoons chopped pitted kalamata olives
1  tablespoon chopped fresh chives
1  tablespoon chopped fresh oregano
1  teaspoon olive oil
¼  pound thinly sliced pepper ham
16  asparagus spears, steamed and chilled (about ¼ pound)
4  (8-inch) fat-free flour tortillas

**1.** Combine first 6 ingredients in a medium bowl. Cover and chill 2 hours. Arrange 1 ounce ham and 4 asparagus spears on each tortilla. Spoon about ⅓ cup cheese mixture over asparagus, and roll up. Yield: 4 servings (serving size: 1 wrap).

CALORIES 230; FAT 7.7g (sat 3.5g, mono 3.2g, poly 0.5g); PROTEIN 13.4g; CARB 26.7g; FIBER 1.8g; CHOL 30mg; IRON 1.9mg; SODIUM 862mg; CALC 130mg

# Black Bean Salsa Pitas

It's best to separately pack the bean mixture, sour cream, bread, and lime wedges. Then assemble the pita halves just before serving.

 1  (15-ounce) can black beans, rinsed and drained
 2  cups finely chopped tomatoes
 1  cup (4 ounces) diced part-skim mozzarella cheese
 ½  cup chopped onion
 ½  cup chopped fresh cilantro
 ¼  cup fresh lime juice (about 2 limes)
 2  tablespoons finely chopped pickled jalapeño peppers
 ½  teaspoon salt
 4  (6-inch) whole wheat pitas, cut in half
 ½  cup reduced-fat sour cream
 1  lime, cut into 4 wedges

**1.** Combine first 8 ingredients in a bowl. Spoon bean mixture evenly into pita halves. Top each with 2 tablespoons sour cream, and serve with lime wedges. Yield: 4 servings (serving size: 2 pita halves).

CALORIES 349; FAT 10.4g (sat 5.7g, mono 1.6g, poly 0.9g); PROTEIN 18.3g; CARB 51.8g; FIBER 9.1g; CHOL 31mg; IRON 3.2mg; SODIUM 960mg; CALC 298mg

Quick Tip: Place a colander in the sink; add beans. Rinse under cold running water and drain well.

# Deluxe Roast Beef Sandwich

For a boost of fiber, pile on the tomatoes and opt for whole grain bread instead of rye bread, which can be just as refined as its white counterpart. (Most whole grain breads are clearly marked as such on the label.) And instead of sipping soda, which is sometimes your only choice at typical lunch joints, reach for a carton of fat-free milk.

  1  tablespoon light mayonnaise
  2  teaspoons prepared horseradish
  2  teaspoons bottled chili sauce
  2  (1-ounce) slices rye bread
  1  romaine lettuce leaf
  3  ounces thinly sliced deli roast beef
  2  (¼-inch-thick) slices tomato
  1  (⅛-inch-thick) slice red onion, separated into rings

**1.** Combine first 3 ingredients. Spread mayonnaise mixture on 1 bread slice. Top with lettuce leaf, roast beef, tomato slices, onion, and remaining bread slice. Yield: 1 serving.

CALORIES 412; FAT 12.7g (sat 4.4g, mono 5.3g, poly 2.9g); PROTEIN 25g; CARB 51.2g; FIBER 5.6g; CHOL 5mg; IRON 4.2mg; SODIUM 1,122mg; CALC 86mg

# Beef-and-Cheese Roll-ups

  1  (6.5-ounce) container light garlic-and-herb cream cheese spread (such as Alouette Lite Garlic and Herb)
  4  (8-inch) 98%-fat-free flour tortillas
  8  curly leaf lettuce leaves
  ¾  pound thinly sliced deli roast beef

**1.** Spread flavored cheese evenly over 1 side of each tortilla; top each evenly with lettuce and roast beef, leaving a ½-inch border around edges.
**2.** Roll up tortillas tightly. Cut in half, and serve immediately; or wrap in plastic wrap, and chill up to 8 hours. Yield: 4 servings (serving size: 1 roll-up).

CALORIES 202; FAT 10.5g (sat 7.1g, mono 1.3g, poly 0.2g); PROTEIN 23.2g; CARB 27.4g; FIBER 1g; CHOL 78.2mg; IRON 2.7mg; SODIUM 1,384mg; CALC 12mg

Make-Ahead Tip: These roll-ups can be made the night before and packed in insulated lunch bags for school or work the next day. Cucumber slices and red onions make great fillers, too.

## Chicken Curry Pitas

- 3 cups chopped roasted skinless, boneless chicken breasts
- 1/3 cup chopped celery
- 1/4 cup low-fat mayonnaise
- 2 tablespoons raisins
- 2 tablespoons hot mango chutney
- 1 tablespoon chopped green onions
- 2 teaspoons fresh lemon juice
- 1 teaspoon curry powder
- 4 (6-inch) pitas, cut in half
- 8 red leaf lettuce leaves

**1.** Combine first 8 ingredients in a medium bowl. Line each pita half with a lettuce leaf. Spoon 1/2 cup chicken mixture into each pita half. Yield: 4 servings (serving size: 2 pita halves).

CALORIES 363; FAT 4.6g (sat 1.2g, mono 1.1g, poly 1g); PROTEIN 33.8g; CARB 47g; FIBER 2.5g; CHOL 75mg; IRON 2.1mg; SODIUM 1,096mg; CALC 90mg

# Lunch Menu

## Roast Chicken-and-Cranberry Sandwiches
### Ripe Tomato Salad *

**\* Combine** 2 tablespoons balsamic vinegar and 2 tablespoons brown sugar; microwave at MEDIUM (50% power) until mixture comes to a boil (about 1½ to 2 minutes). Let stand until cool and slightly thick (about 5 minutes). Place ¾ cup salad greens on each of 4 plates. Slice 1 large yellow and 1 large red tomato; arrange on top of salad greens. Sprinkle ¼ teaspoon salt evenly over tomatoes. Drizzle with vinaigrette. Sprinkle evenly with 1 tablespoon pine nuts, if desired.

Quick Tip: To dissolve sugar in liquid, cook the mixture in the microwave for 1 to 2 minutes or just until it comes to a boil. This beats having to stir the mixture constantly until the granules disappear.

## Roast Chicken-and-Cranberry Sandwiches

¼   cup (2 ounces) ⅓-less-fat cream cheese, softened
¼   cup bottled cranberry chutney (such as Crosse & Blackwell)
 8   (1-ounce) slices multigrain bread
½   cup thinly sliced radishes
½   cup trimmed arugula or spinach
 2   cups chopped roasted skinless, boneless chicken breasts

**1.** Combine cream cheese and chutney in a small bowl. Spread 1 tablespoon cream cheese mixture over each bread slice. Arrange one-fourth of radishes, arugula, and chicken on each of 4 bread slices. Top with remaining bread slices. Yield: 4 servings (serving size: 1 sandwich).

CALORIES 361; FAT 9.1g (sat 3.6g, mono 3.2g, poly 1.2g); PROTEIN 30.3g; CARB 39.7g; FIBER 3.2g; CHOL 76mg; IRON 2.7mg; SODIUM 459mg; CALC 63mg

# Cobb Salad Pitas

Who says a salad has to be eaten from a bowl? Instead, stuff the salad mixture inside a whole wheat pita half for a quick-and-easy handheld lunch.

  1  (12-ounce) package American-style lettuce blend
1½  cups coarsely chopped smoked turkey breast (about 6 ounces)
  ⅓  cup bottled real bacon bits
  ⅓  cup low-fat blue cheese dressing
  4  whole wheat pitas, cut in half
  8  cherry tomatoes, halved
  2  chopped green onions

**1.** Combine first 4 ingredients in a medium bowl; toss well.
**2.** Fill each pita half with lettuce mixture. Top with cherry tomatoes and green onions. Yield: 4 servings (serving size: 2 pita halves).

CALORIES 283; FAT 5.7g (sat 0.9g, mono 1.4g, poly 1.2g); PROTEIN 18.6g; CARB 42.1g; FIBER 6.6g; CHOL 23mg; IRON 3.6mg; SODIUM 1,237mg; CALC 59mg

# Turkey Roll-ups

Packed with protein and low in calories, these roll-ups allow you to wrap and go! Try them with a sliced apple dipped in low-fat caramel sauce.

  2  tablespoons light cream cheese with chives and onion
  4  (6-inch) pitas
  4  (1-ounce) slices deli turkey
  1  small red bell pepper, thinly sliced

**1.** Spread 2 tablespoons cream cheese over each pita. Top each with 1 turkey slice and pepper strips. Roll up, and wrap in wax paper. Yield: 4 servings (serving size: 1 roll-up).

CALORIES 212; FAT 2.4g (sat 1.1g, mono 0.2g, poly 0.4g); PROTEIN 11g; CARB 36g; FIBER 1.7g; CHOL 15mg; IRON 2.2mg; SODIUM 697mg; CALC 68mg

## Lunch Menu

**SERVES 4**

### Turkey-Vegetable Wraps

Tangy Coleslaw *

***Combine** ¼ cup low-fat mayonnaise, ¼ cup plain fat-free yogurt, 1½ tablespoons sugar, 2 teaspoons prepared horseradish, 1 teaspoon dry mustard, and ¼ teaspoon salt. Toss with half of a 16-ounce package cabbage-and-carrot coleslaw; cover and chill.

## Turkey-Vegetable Wraps

- 2   cups coarsely chopped smoked turkey breast (about 8 ounces)
- 2   cups gourmet salad greens
- ½   cup fresh corn kernels (about 1 ear)
- ½   cup chopped red bell pepper
- ¼   cup thinly sliced green onions
- 3   tablespoons light ranch dressing
- 4   (8-inch) flour tortillas

**1.** Combine first 6 ingredients in a large bowl, tossing well to coat. Warm tortillas according to package directions. Top each tortilla with 1 cup turkey mixture; roll up. Yield: 4 servings (serving size: 1 wrap).

CALORIES 252; FAT 7.2g (sat 1.2g, mono 2.3g, poly 3.3g); PROTEIN 18.2g; CARB 29.8g; FIBER 3g; CHOL 32mg; IRON 2.4mg; SODIUM 741mg; CALC 46mg

Quick Tip: Using prepackaged salad greens cuts down on the preparation time required.

# Smoked Turkey–Cream Cheese
# Bagel Sandwiches

Toast each bagel before making these sandwiches, and enjoy the extra crunch at lunchtime. The protein from the ham, turkey, and cheese prepares you for the remainder of the workday.

2 tablespoons (1 ounce) tub-style fat-free cream cheese
4 large pitted kalamata olives, chopped
4 (3.4-ounce) whole wheat bagels, sliced in half
4 curly leaf lettuce leaves
4 (½-ounce) slices smoked ham
4 (1-ounce) slices smoked turkey breast
2 ounces reduced-fat Havarti cheese, thinly sliced
2 thin slices red onion
4 slices ripe tomato (about 1 small)
¼ ripe avocado, cut into 4 very thin slices

**1.** Combine cream cheese and olives.
**2.** Spread olive spread evenly over bottom half of each bagel.
**3.** Place lettuce leaves over spread; layer ham, turkey, and cheese on lettuce. Separate onion slices into rings, and divide evenly among sandwiches. Add tomato and avocado slices. Cover with remaining bagel halves. Yield: 4 servings (serving size: 1 sandwich).

CALORIES 380; FAT 7.7g (sat 1g, mono 1.8g, poly 0.9g); PROTEIN 22.7g; CARB 60.5g; FIBER 10.5g; CHOL 20mg; IRON 3.8mg; SODIUM 1,029mg; CALC 159mg

Quick Tip: The easiest way to pit an avocado is to slice all the way around the pit and through both ends of the fruit with a chef's knife. Then twist the halves in opposite directions, and pull them apart. Tap the pit sharply with the knife, and twist the blade to lift the pit.

# Lunch Menu

**SERVES 4**

## Lentil-Tomato Soup
melba toast with light garlic-and-herb cream cheese spread
honeydew melon

## Lentil-Tomato Soup

This delicious soup is quite versatile: It makes a big batch and freezes well.
So you're assured many lunches from this recipe.

 1   tablespoon olive oil
 2   cups chopped onion
 1   teaspoon ground turmeric
 1   teaspoon ground cumin
 1   teaspoon chili powder
 1   teaspoon ground red pepper
 $\frac{1}{4}$   teaspoon salt
 $\frac{1}{4}$   teaspoon black pepper
 2   garlic cloves, minced
 $3\frac{1}{3}$   cups water
 $2\frac{1}{3}$   cups dried lentils
 $\frac{1}{3}$   cup chopped fresh cilantro
 3   (14-ounce) cans fat-free, less-sodium chicken broth
 1   (28-ounce) can diced tomatoes, undrained
Chopped fresh tomatoes (optional)
Cilantro sprigs (optional)

**1.** Heat oil in a large Dutch oven over medium-high heat. Add onion; sauté
3 minutes or until tender. Add turmeric and next 6 ingredients; sauté 1 minute.
Add $3\frac{1}{3}$ cups water and next 4 ingredients; bring to a boil. Reduce heat;
simmer 1 hour.
**2.** Reserve 2 cups lentil mixture. Place half of remaining mixture in a blender;
process until smooth. Pour pureed soup into a large bowl. Repeat procedure
with other half of remaining mixture. Stir in reserved 2 cups lentil mixture.
Garnish with chopped tomatoes and cilantro sprigs, if desired. Yield:
11 servings (serving size: 1 cup).

CALORIES 186; FAT 1.9g (sat 0.3g, mono 1.0g, poly 0.4g); PROTEIN 14.1g; CARB 29.8g; FIBER 13.9g; CHOL 0mg; IRON 4.4mg;
SODIUM 412mg; CALC 54mg

# Chipotle Red-and-White Bean Chili

Serve this tasty chili with baked tortilla chips, carrot and celery sticks, and ranch dressing.

  1  cup frozen chopped onion
 ½  pound reduced-fat pork sausage
  1  green bell pepper, chopped
  1  red bell pepper, chopped
  1  (1.25-ounce) package 30%-less-sodium taco seasoning mix (such as McCormick's)
  1  (14.5-ounce) can Mexican-style diced tomatoes, drained
  1  (8-ounce) can no-salt-added tomato sauce
  1  (15-ounce) can no-salt-added light red kidney beans, rinsed and drained
  1  (19-ounce) can cannellini beans or other white beans, rinsed and drained
  2  chipotle chiles in adobo sauce, seeded and chopped plus 2 teaspoons adobo sauce
  1  cup chopped fresh cilantro

**1.** Cook onion, sausage, and peppers in a nonstick skillet over medium-high heat until sausage is browned and vegetables are tender, stirring to crumble sausage.
**2.** Drain sausage mixture; return to pan. Add seasoning mix and next 5 ingredients. Bring mixture to a boil; cover and simmer 5 minutes. Stir in cilantro just before serving. Yield: 4 servings (serving size 1¾ cups).

CALORIES 432; FAT 11.4g (sat 3.7g, mono 0.1g, poly 0.4g); PROTEIN 23.2g; CARB 57.4g; FIBER 12.3g; CHOL 40mg; IRON 6.5mg; SODIUM 1,151mg; CALC 116mg